Blind Boy Fuller   MISSISSIPPI FRED McDOWELL

Charlie Musselwhite   Sippie Wallace

Jelly Roll Morton

Ivory Joe Hunter   Otis Spann

MAGIC SLIM

Mance Lipscomb

JIMMY ROGERS

Jay McShann   HOUND DOG TAYLOR

Lil Green   BUKKA WHITE

Otis Rush

Little Walter   Bobby "Blue" Bland   Sonny Boy Williamson

Robert Lockwood Jr.   Howlin' Wolf

Johnny Copeland

Junior Wells

Sleepy John Estes   ROBERT CRAY

Albert Collins   Ethel Waters   Bobby Rush

Taj Mahal

Louisiana Red   CLARENCE "GATEMOUTH" BROWN

Etta James   W.C. Handy   Josh White

Rufus Thomas

Son Seals   KEB' MO'   Odetta   Charley Patton

Guy Davis   Koko Taylor   CRIPPLE CLARENCE LOFTON

Otis Taylor   Skip James   Memphis Minnie

ALVIN YOUNGBLOOD HART

MISSISSIPPI JOHN HURT

"BLIND" LEMON JEFFERSON   "BLIND" WILLIE JOHNSON

Huddie "Lead Belly" Ledbetter

ROOTS and BLUES

ARNOLD ADOFF

ROOTS and BLUES

A CELEBRATION

Paintings by R. GREGORY CHRISTIE

CLARION BOOKS

Houghton Mifflin Harcourt | New York • Boston

For:

Virginia Esther Hamilton Adoff
              Sitting   L o n g
              Into That   Room
              On   East Second
                        Street:
Twelve String
     D r e a d
   N a u g h t
Always
Insistent
Behind That Glorious   Voice
          That Shining   Face.

Could   She Not   S a n g.

     S h e   S a n g.

          — A.A.

To the McCullough family—Diego, Jonah,
Freddy, and Elvira ("S u n s h i n e").

          — R.G.C.

Each Word A Hammer Hit. Each Word The Solid Tip

*of finger hitting squarely on to the center of the ivory
yellow piano key. E a c h hammer to each steel wire hit
makes tone makes sound and resonates: rings like rocks
hitting calm water. C i r c l e s of sounds reach out
like circles of words: flow stories out from the shore.*

*I look into the water and see my usual face bending out
and under the ripples: bending as blue notes extend
from finger tip to steel wire hit to air to ear to memory.*

Go Forward. Go Back. There I s Always Time.

There was always time. There was dripdripdrip
of rain from side of branch to tip of twig
to covering on roof. There   was   great wail
of childbirthing and high-pitched ha ha laughs.

Some hundreds of years a g o some afternoon:
the   f o o t   f a l l s   on the forest   floor,
the   f o o t   f a l l s   on dry branch. Cracks:
some sharp break sound   some pop ping w o o d
                                        s t a c c a t o into
                                                        the
                                                        air.

Seeds Fall In Footprints And Spring Up Grow

almost overnight into songs: the earth water
                                                            a i r
                                                            hot
                                                            sun
shapes and steels and strengthens
                        i n t o permanence.

Chained

in rags in blood in dark death of daylight.
To survive the passage across the ocean from
life to living hell to life in hell means
                                    silent
                                    singing
                                    of old
                                    s o n g s.
Behind the eyes
the fingers strum
homeland strings and memory of my history
                    remains as strong as steel.

Always: this melody of words is journey home.

Listening:

*This many words machine-gunned through close air
and sacred chanting across the Caribbean waters.
Brown fingers moving with the regularity of rhythm
onto stretched skins onto smooth carved w o o d.*

This new world music m o v e s with shackle sounds.

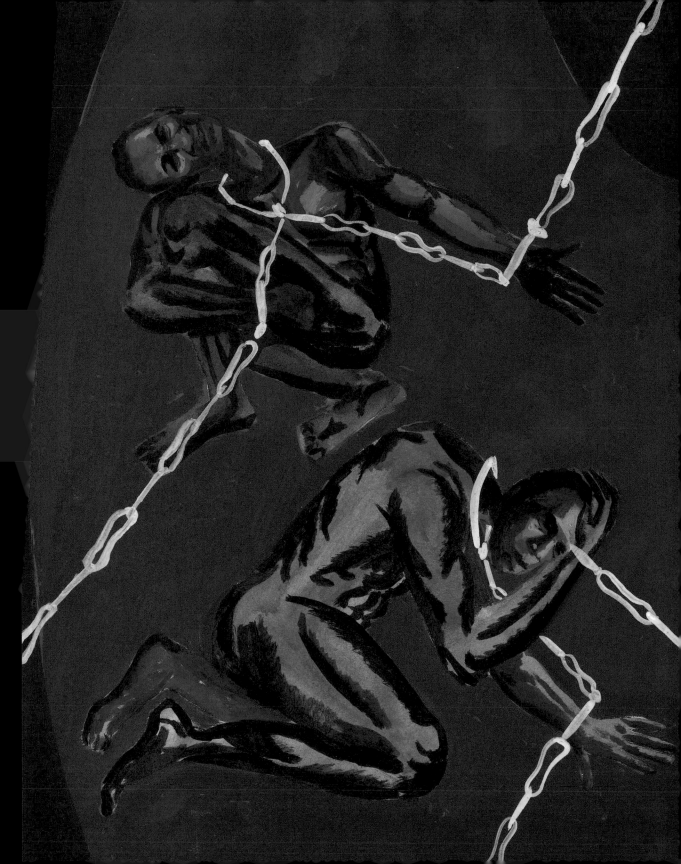

From Africa   And   Caribbean   Shores

to those t i m e s of d i r t floors
and the blood of mothers: moving
from c o t t o n fields a n d flooded
rice acres   we   arrive at the time
of morning greetings of   b i r d s.

The g r i o t cackles as the story
ends   and   the   p l a n t a t i o n
w h i p s crack high   into   treble
lines of lines of lines:
                                s i n g i n g
deeper than the story of the song.

Listening:

Can you hear the ancestor words
still in echo over oceans a n d
                    c e n t u r i e s?
Into this room:
        each
        call
        the
        chords
        we use
        to
        make
        our
        songs.

The Giant Ice Mountains Slide South

then ice becomes water and water moves
in its rush to rise   into its   returning.
But the black dirt and red clay remain.

Down In The Delta   As Sure As River Rises

floods and falls: the   notes   are   passed   along.
Chords and harmonies on front porches contain the
songs that move beyond river mud and rotting wood.

Engineers Of Memory Kept Plans During Generations.

This hollow log   this discarded box   conceal each
blueprint of beats   words   the h i s t o r y o f
                                    f e e l i n g s.

Listening:

Who was here cutting down Delta forest trees
burning stumps on hot afternoons? Under the
                                        brush
                                          of
                                centuries:
the richest black bottom river land.

Swamps And Smells Old River Floods Just Mud.

Prisons and chain gangs and cotton fields and
dogs howling on moonless nights and guards

                                                            and
                                                            dogs
                                                            and
                                                            dogs
                                                            and
                                                            dogs
                                                            and
                                                            dogs.

We Want To Think

some magic birds
flew   over slave
                    ships
that long
              time   ago,
their
beaks beat music
              time: old
                    stories
tucked
    under   feathers.

But stories play themselves inside heads
and rest with song and memory of villages:
all instruments of ceremony t r a v e l
                                    w i t h
                                    t h e m.
Their fingers carve secret music
                    in the air.

O n e   M o r e   R i v e r.

The black crow tells the
                               red
                              bird
                              and
                               the
                               red
                              bird
                        tells the
                             robin
and the robin
g a t h e r s
her   robin
       babies
          and   tells   the
                      old
                    story.

First   there   was   the   great   ocean.
And then there is this m u d d y
river flooding fields. Now smell the
fresh wet breeze just past this hill:
just past those trees to the north.

Listening:

Hit stick to stick.
Hit hollow   l o g.
Hit an old   b o x.
Hit spoon to spoon.
Hit spoon to spoon
                to thigh.
Hit
leg.
Hit
leg.
Hit
leg.

Curses In The Night Resound Through Years

into the tops of trees: into   the   very   sky.
Under the hot sun: t h e   c h o p   c h o p
                                                    hoe
measures out the beats of freedom.

Listening:

This bird on branch next to village path to home.

The high-metal shuffle of chains between wrists.
A hoe hits rock hits rock in Georgia ground.
Hoe cake pan hits side of iron stove each morning.
Rasping s l i d e of ropes a r o u n d trees.
Hooves ring steel-on-stone over cobbled streets.

S p l a s h of river fish on Alabama afternoons.

Blues Songs Flow Like Rivers Can C u t Through Rock:

can shape and change shape can go in all directions.
Like mother tongue ma ma sounds: they are always
recognized with s m i l e s and outstretched fingers.

Remember The Red.

                    B l u e s
                    f r o m
                        red
memories:
bright   b l o o d
                    d a r k
                        t o
                    b r o w n
                    a f t e r
                    d e a t h,
                        and
                        the
                    r i c h
                        red
                    c h i l d
                    b i r t h
                    c o l o r
                        o f
                    j o y.

Remember the first
                    music:
                    the first
                        cry.

The
Mississippi   River

is
an   African   river.
Black American mud.
Black American t o e
                and
                t a p
                and
                song.
This   blues:
this   black
        blues
          river
          flows
back
ward.

An African   river.
An African   people
in   American m u d:
              s i n g
                i n g
              s o m e
          h i g h e r
          g r o u n d
              s o n g.

Mechesebe.

Long before blue songs was brown river.
                        Always the river.
                        Big Muddy.
                        F a t h e r
                                o f
                        W a t e r s.
                        M i s s i s si p p i.
P l a n t a t i o n s
like   S t o v a l l.
            Then
clusters of stores,
                then
                more
                h o u s e s,
                then
                t o w n s: G r e e n v i l l e
                            C l a r k s d a l e
                                    i t t y
                                    b i t t y
                                    I t t a
                                    B e n a.

                        Missis sippi.

You Have To Love The People Building Roads

laying brick building machines through   smoke
and steam: blue music through the good and bad
                                                and
                                             simple
                                                 in
                                          between.

S i n g i n g:

I f   t h e c h a i n b r e a k s
before t h e   r o c k   b r e a k s
        s t i l l   n o t free.

        When I finish this road
        s t i l l   can't   ride.
        When I finish that road
        s t i l l   step   aside.
        When I build this house
        s t i l l   need   a key.
        When I build that house
        s t i l l   not for   me.

I f   t h e c h a i n b r e a k s
before t h e   r o c k   b r e a k s
        s t i l l   n o t free.

              N o t free.

              Free.

Just Folks.

For longer than the cotton has been growing in the fields
the streets are mud and gravel depending on season and weather.
People just live here and work at what they can and try
to feed their kids and buy shoes and dream their dreams and songs.

Working the music is like working the dirt: rows of fields
through years each daylight hour and long nights of misty light.
From eyes to mouth to ears to fingers is the same simple circle
as breath in and breath out: as automatic as foot taps on floor.

Sip some cool water and think about red sunsets and the next days.

Listening:

Hands are banging two tin cans out in the alleyway.
The tea kettle whistles long into the hot afternoon.
Mosquitoes buzz your ears. Flies march along your arm.

Soft cannelcoal and wet wood strips
pop inside the old black iron stove.
Your lips whistle into hot tea steam.

Kiss me now.

The Kerosene Lamp Is Smoking Up The Night Room

and the smell of burning firewood   s l i d e s
out the cracks in the cabin walls: a n d t h e
                                          n i g h t
                                          m u s i c
                                          s l i d e s
over   the   windowsills.

Stories   become   sighs:
and a voice   so   light
                so   light
                so   lightly
hums   some
a l m o s t   words.

Memory   s i n g s   hope.

S o m e t i m e s:

It is only the joy shining out of your eyes
that gives me the strength   to chop this ground
so far beyond the dead tired muscles in my arms.

S o m e t i m e s:

It is only the insistent cry out of the mouth
of this beautiful baby that gives me strength
to turn the other cheek and work to buy the milk.

Singing finger pops to kisses: you can hug
                    me into h o m e m a d e
                              b i s c u i t s

                    u n t i l the d a r k
                         c l o u d s
                              r o l l
                              a w a y.

Listening:

Those feet on   fall season   fallen leaves.
Those feet shuffling through pine needles.
Those feet running down dark New Orleans streets
             reaching ship before   first tide sail.
St e a m
whistles
c e l e b r a t e
the rising   o f
             t h e
             s u n.

Ma Ma

washes my face at night and fills my bowl.
That page of paper hidden under the mattress is
my reading book. She tells stories in whispers
and teaches with her sighs. Her songs arecircles
of light beyond kerosene and candles.   W e
                                          d r e a m
                                             t h e
                                          m u s i c
                                              o f
                                          b e t t e r
                                          t i m e s.

Listening:

Dolls out of strips of old shirt cloth and carved wood tops
just lie on the ground until cool breeze stirs branches:
                              until the   sticks beating floors
                                    and walls and tree trunks

call rhythms
   d a n c i n g
              i n
         s t i l l
            a i r.

44

L i s t e n i n g:

Bold bursting burp from a full stomach.
The thin stream of steam from the single egg
cracked at the edge of the saucer: of the

                                                cup.

A spoon stirs against the sides
of a glass and the thinnest flake
of brown-gold croissant f a l l s
to the plate between our smiles.

Listening:

*The long gray grandmother hair falling
onto starched-lace shoulders and the hot
peppers are just beginning to pop and pop.*

*Her high laugh still floats out the window
over the river the bay the ocean: years.*

*T o p
notes
carry
h o m e
t h i s
s o n g.*

The Grands: Grand Grand Grandmothers. Mothers:

                                    the mothers
keening smiles telling   listening
kissalwayskiss: singing that blue
                            song.

Echoes of strongsongs and weak requests out
                                      her
kitchen window and off the porch steps:
still ripple between syllables of bone.

On the high hill path the   yodeling,
and under the tent some sparkledressed
woman named S m i t h knows her well.

Listening:

Grocery store cash register rings,
and dollar bills go f l o a t i n g
onto l a n d l o r d tables e a c h
                                    w e e k,
                                    e a c h
                                    m o n t h.

Coins wrapped in head
scarves: tied   tight
and h i d d e n o u t
            of s i g h t.

The Rising Sounds Of Singing From The Big

white church must meet in each Sunday
sky with insisting ancestor drums.

Listening:

Scattering mouse feet
g u n shots   laughter
fluttering closing
                        eye
                    lids:
fingers popping.
Hands clapping.
Hands clapping.
Voices   shouting.
        Shouting
a m e n
a m e n.

Amen.

Lonnie Johnson And Son House And Charlie Patton

playing   joints   from   Missis sippi to Arkansas
to: justbackagain. ClarksdaletoRosedale   to   Itta
Bena to Marianna to Marvell to Sun day morning
sleep:
    to old roads north and north and north.

Juke Joints   Or Jook Joints   Or Joints   For Dancing

into morning: Purple Rain Lounge and Club Cat Man
and Club Amnesia and Club Chill and Blue Diamond.

Listening:

Sweet smiling Gertrude Pridgett "Ma" Rainey begins
totap that left foot forward toward the front r o w
                                   a n d
                                   a n d
heads nod   eyes raise up s h o u t s.
W h i s p e r s of   a g r e e m e n t.
                                   H e r
                                   m a n
                                   g o n e.

Each
Time.

Give me the shuffle the waltz the march
             the twelve bars of feet sliding
             almost to the end of the accent
             of the beat. Saved by s p a c e
             b e t w e e n b e a t s: o u r
                                      always
                                       time
                                        of
                                       toes

         and fingers pop
                pop

                PPP
                i i i
                nnn
                ggg
                . . .

Robert Johnson:

his   fingertips
always   just
right   on steel
strings.   His
words   cutting
through   thick
smoke   true
as   breathing.

He was so head-and-shoulders grand. They said he sold
his soul   to the eternal-infernal-dark-suit-salesman   one
devil of a night: some crossroads somewhere s o u t h of
Memphis   near   the great river. We can still tell that
story and smile as we sing his words. His soul is in
his songs and his songs live deep on blue e a r t h.

W. C.

Dandy
Handy
flies   down
              from
Saint
Louis   for
              the
              day
and
his   a r m s
are   j u s t
      p l a i n
      t i r e d.

A
mud
song melody
sticks
inside   his
      bowler
              hat
a l l
t h e
way   back
              north
              to his
      g l o r y.

Walking
T h e n
Sitting:

resting on chair after long day of work.
        This hum this buzz: finally some
                           words
     pop
     o u t into air of the room.
     The song takes form makes
                      s e n s e
                      makes
                      t h e s e
                      goose
                      bumps
                      c h i l l
   the back of neck
   the length of arms: always
                      f e e l
                      better
                      f a s t.

Blues Harp Called Mouth Organ Called Blues Harp

called

harp   called h a r m o n i c a. With hands
without hands with breathing   m o u t h
and wire it to a cage around your neck and
keep your hands free   for the guitar.   Just
breathing the s o n g
the b e a t
within the
s o n g.
Breathing
strong.

Climbing To The Top Of The Hill

I can see   all the way across
              the Delta
              t o t h e   bending
                        river.

Inside my head:
behind my eyes
I can see   s o u t h   in all
              d i r e c t i o n s.

Th   i   s
summer
a   i   r: thick with humidity   thick with summer smells
              thick with cascades   of   flies   rolling   down
                                    from   cooler   currents
              thick with memories   of bending summer sounds.

              Blues   bends   branches   in the   summer   trees.
              Blues   is curling around   my sister's braids.
              Blues   is k n o c k i n g   o n   the   d o o r
                                    o f the neighbor
                                              l a d y:

              b o r row i n g   s o m e   s u g a r.

64

Muddy Waters Steps Down

on

t o

that

Chicago

t r a i n

s t a t i o n

p l a t f o r m

with a suitcase

of Mississippi

R i v e r

with a suitcase

of Mississippi

D e l t a

with a suitcase

of Mississippi

dripping

on side

w a l k

s.

L o n g

n i g h t

s o u n d s

b o u n c i n g

b e t w e e n

b u i l d i n g

s.

On The Porch On That Black Street.

D e t r o i t: Johnny Lee Hooker
                those evenings
                                    with
                Muddy Waters   and
                                    Bee
                                    Bee
                                    Bee
                                    Bee.

                Do I imagine   Miss
                               i s s
                               i p p
                               i
                               i
                               i
                               mud
        o n
        t h e   b o t t o m
                        o f
                        y o u r
                        p a n t s
                        l e g s

                        s t i l l?

You Know You Never Miss The Water.

The refrigerator	is full of good food.
The refrigerator	is empty long before
	the end of the month.
The h o u s e	is t o a s t warm.
The h o u s e	is m u c h too cold
	even under blankets.

You know you must remember to always
                                    k e e p
                                    a full
                                    j a r
                                    of hugs
                    on the top shelf, s o m e
                                    e x t r a
                                    k i s s e s
                    in the b o t t o m drawer.

You know you never   miss   the water,
                    never   miss   the water,
                    never   miss   the water:
                              till the   well
                                    runs
                                    dry.

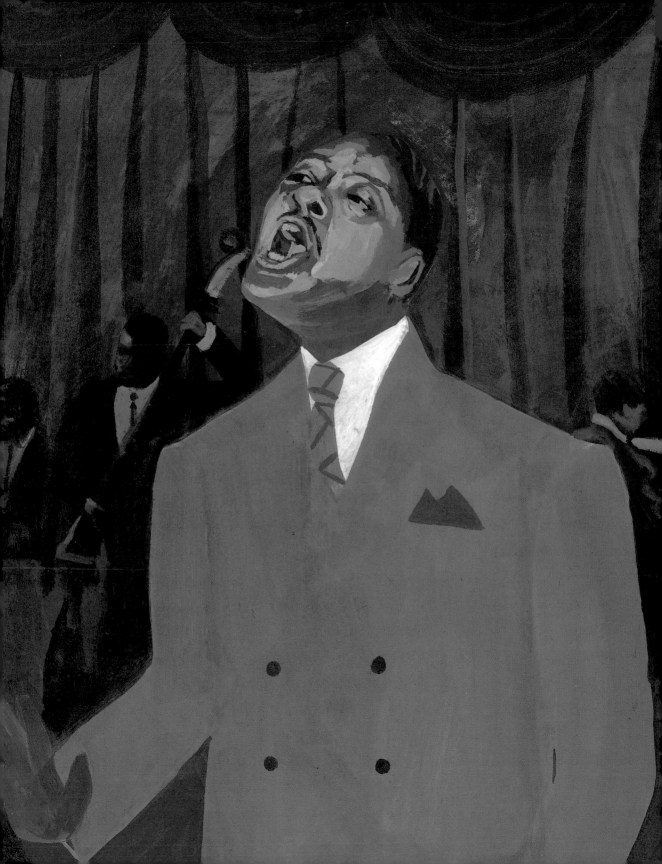

At The Moment The Spotlight Hits Him

standing up so tall   his head is almost
                          into   next   week:
                          his   chest   puffed
                                   almost
                          p a s t   bursting
                                   buttons.
N o w:
o n e   deep   breath
o n e   deep   breath
o n e   deep   breath so hard   it   makes
                          me   stop
                          my mouth
                                   pop
                          my   eyes.
N o w:
o n e   long   expulsion
o n e   long   expulsion
o n e   long   bursting
                   bursting
                   burst of
                   breath of song of   breath.
              A breath of beginning   blue.

G o i n g   to   C h i c a g o
G o i n g   to   C h i c a g o   oh   baby
G o i n g   to   C h i c a g o: *singing*
                          so   sorry
                                   that
                          I can't
                                   take
                          y o u.

Kansas City.

Big Joe Turner in a dark gray suit
some dark nights in
suchbright lights
talking love:
de

man

  d

ing   love. Wailing when
                    it goes:
                    so

                    so   sad.
              Wailing
                    as love
        returns: his
                    voice

                    can

                    make

                    you

                    smile
        through taste of
                    tears.

Our American Castles

are
the funky blue clubs
        and concert halls
        and s t r e e t s
from
the
Crescent City   to K.C.
to Chicago   to Harlem.

Piano benches are our
American thrones: some
raised platform back
of a long room is
coronation   central
                    for
                    the
                    king
                    queen
                    voices
t h a t r u l e
f r o m t h e n
t o   n o w
t o a l w a y s.

Clapton And Stevie Ray And Now At Our Time

                                        in this world.
                                        This
                                        blue black
                                        magic:
f l i e s f r o m   mouths
to ears f r o m   p a s t
to just l a s t   n i g h t.

Bayous are wheat fields aremountains are   steel
bridgesare blacktop blue(s) highways are oceans
are continents are circles of satellites unseen.

We can see the kids still sitting on frontporch
steps   see the kids at suburb malls   seethekids
floating in inevitable tides of bottleneckglass.

Eyes a r e c l o s e d
        a n d fin g ers
              m o v e
              b e y o n d
              m e r e
              c o l o r s
              i n t o
              l o v e.

Bessie And Alberta And Victoria And Trixie

and Memphis Minnie and S i s t e r
                            R o s e t t a
and W i l l i eM a e   B i gM a m a
                            K o k o
                            K o k o
                                  o
                                  o.
                            G o
                            b a c k.
                            G o
                            forward:

to Dinah and Billie and Ruth
        and Sarah   and Maci
        and Phoebe and t h a t
                            wet
                            sweat
                            woman
giving answers to her
                            first
                            name
                            basis.

Aunts and cousins come visit everyday.

Sit Up S t r a i g h t And S i n g.

Stand up. The blues are in your spine:
hard as shackle steel   soft as fingers
picking l i n e s   from steel strings.

Old as that scratchy voice on some old
recording cylinder   and young as baby
sleeping sound: we sing each morning
sunrise s t r o n g e r than yesterday.

We Are Out Here This Early Spring Evening

quiet for a moment.
All the stories ended.
Through t h e window
the music of some man
is singing freedom.
The man
wakes
o n e
morning
a n d
h i s
m i n d
i s
o n
freedom.

We look out over our fields to the trees
at the edge of the yard. I can almost
see over the trees and through the trees
to the edge of our town and over the
hills to the river: the last edge of Ohio.

Calls and curses still punctuate the song.
Past time and the river was our beginning.
Shivers on this chill night make us laugh.
We are inside our present t i m e of hugs.
When the song is ended we sleep safe.

Listening:

Singing vegetables for sale near Auction Square.
Silence under heavy snow one Kansas City winter.
M e m p h i s   w a t e r f r o n t   noise and rush.
Saint   Louis   w a t e r f r o n t   noise and rush.
C h i c a g o   l a k e   f r o n t :
                    w a t e r f r o n t   noise and rush.
Long nights.
Long nights.
Long nights.

Long years.
Long years.
Long years.

One
Hop

from cotton gin
                          in
past times
to
fast
car streets
s i n g i n g:

hip

deep
in   blues.

A l w a y s.

Break my heart.
Break my heart and I can still live.
Break my heart and I can walk around that tree.
Break my heart and I can still feel rain on face.

>How   can
>loss of love
>   and
>empty belly
>   and
>night   howl
>animals and
>train   ride
>north   and
>once   again
>   e m p t y:

break my heart for good and real and true
when tomorrow almost smiles through the doorway
at first light of dawn and the cold wind hits my
face with that promise of warmer   spring breezes.

And we have always sung about hearts and healing
broken pieces into new and beating creations when
eyes open   to first light of morning sun shining
>in my b a c k d o o r
>   shining
>in my b a c k d o o r.
>   Shining
>   shining:

a l w a y s.

Blue Line Runs Straight.

If the old cigar box is warped and water-stained
or the store-bought electric creation gleams
in   multicolored   spotlights:

                                        the   line   runs
                                        straight as some
                                        sad arrow to the
                                        loving   heart.

Train tracks and bus ride
blacktop late each night:
from camp ground to smallest
town t o a l l   the cities.

N o w i n o u r t i m e this world sings blue.

Take A Single Black Pencil

and draw this line that shows the man is sitting
in his straight-backed chair m o u t h open,
arms cradling guitar: his fingers pressing and
picking a single l i n e of clean-as-a-knife-
through-marshmallow-soup n o t e s that circle
his head in final fall to join his tapping foot.

You can take a single black pencil and draw that
                                            line
straight from last night's laugh
ris ing t o to mor row's stars.

Inside This Circle Of Blue.

Inside
these
words
inside   this repeating of
words   this repeating of
      this   singing
         circle   of   b l u e:
                             i s
                          t h i s
         circle   of   living
         h e r e o n   moving
         circle   of   moving
         r o c k in s p a c e.
Red
blood
of
birth: the color of the rising sun
        the color of the fading sun
        i n t o   d a r k n e s s.

Now mix these colors for our songs.

E a c h   W o r d *The Down Stroke Of Callused Fingers*

on taut strings. *E a c h w o r d* the crack of stick
on sharp steel rim of *s n a r e:* cutting through
the rocksolid fourfour *f o u r. E a c h w o r d a s*

clear as gravel lying still on river bottom beneath so
s h i m m e r i n g water: round stones through layers
of reflected light   through the history of the water.

E a c h   w o r d: this true-to-bone moment sliding out
beyond story beyond mud and cotton even beyond love.

Each word repeated: always expected always a surprise.

CLARION BOOKS
215 Park Avenue South, New York, New York 10003

Text copyright © 2011 by
Arnold Adoff
Illustrations copyright © 2011 by
R. Gregory Christie

The text of this book was set in 17-point Grit Primer.
The paintings were executed in acrylic paint.
Book design by Sharismar Rodriguez

Clarion Books is an imprint of
Houghton Mifflin Harcourt Publishing Company.

www.hmhbooks.com

Library of Congress Cataloging-in-Publication Data
Adoff, Arnold.
Roots and blues : a celebration / by Arnold Adoff ; illustrated by R. Gregory Christie.
p. cm.
Summary: Lyrical text explores how Blues have been part of everyday life throughout history,
from its origins in the sounds of the earth, through slaves' voices singing of freedom,
to today's greatest performers—and listeners.

ISBN 978-0-547-23554-7

1. Blues (Music)—Poetry. 2. African Americans—Music—Poetry. 3. Music—Poetry.
[1. Novels in verse.] I. Christie, Gregory, 1971– ill. II. Title.

PS3551.D66R66 2010
811'.54—dc22
2009026625

Manufactured in China
LEO 10 9 8 7 6 5 4 3 2
4500287110

B.B. KING Son House BIG BILL BROONZY Albert King

Sonny Terry Peetie Wheatstraw

T-Bone Walker Ruth Brown Champion Jack Dupree

Dinah Washington Sonny Boy Williamson

Brownie McGhee Bessie Smith Tampa Red

Wynonie Harris Louis Jordan Lightnin' Hopkins

Memphis Slim Muddy Waters

REVEREND GARY DAVIS Jimmy Witherspoon

Ray Charles

Furry Lewis BO Diddley

James Cotton Carey Bell

PINETOP PERKINS Victoria Spivey

JOHN LEE HOOKER

Ma Rainey Magic Sam David "Honeyboy" Edwards

ROBERT JOHNSON Jimmy Rushing

J.B. Hutto

Buddy Guy Willie Dixon Lonnie Johnson

Elmore James

Big Joe Turner James Brown Stevie Ray Vaughan

Eric Clapton Alberta Hunter

Blind Willie McTell Sister Rosetta Tharpe